You hear many reasons why marriages and long-term relationships break up, but there's one that's seldom acknowledged: Many committed couples would get along better if only they weren't roommates.

But what can they do? They have to share a home, don't they?

What if they chose to defy expectations—their own and everyone else's? What if they decided to live in separate apartments or houses, nearby or even side-by-side? Wouldn't they avoid many tensions that typically drag couples down? Wouldn't they gain richer and happier times together?

Anne L. Watson and her partner have lived this kind of life successfully for nearly two decades. In this ground-breaking book, she draws on personal experience to reveal the benefits of such an arrangement and tell how you might make it work for yourself. In the end, Anne helps you understand that not all couples need a common residence to live happily ever after.

> "Wise, timely, and truthful . . . There are as many ways of living together as there are people, and it's great that there's at last a book reflecting that with such humour and insight."—Deborah Moggach, author, *The Best Exotic Marigold Hotel* and *Tulip Fever*

Also by Anne L. Watson

Novels

Skeeter: A Cat Tale ~ Pacific Avenue ~ Joy ~ Flight ~ Cassie's Castaways ~ Willow's Crystal ~ Benecia's Mirror ~ A Chambered Nautilus ~ Departure

Crafts & Homemaking

Smart Housekeeping ~ Baking with Cookie Molds ~ Cookie Molds Around the Year ~ Smart Soapmaking ~ Milk Soapmaking ~ Smart Lotionmaking ~ Castile Soapmaking ~ Cool Soapmaking

LIVING

APART

TOGETHER

A Unique Path to Marital Happiness
OR
The Joy of Sharing Lives Without
Sharing an Address

Anne L. Watson

Shepard Publications
Friday Harbor, Washington

Version 1.1

Contents

The Vow

I, _____, take you, _____, to be my lawfully wedded (husband/wife), to have and to hold, from this day forward, for better, for worse, for richer, for poorer, in sickness and in health, until death do us part.

This is a common, traditional form of the wedding vow.

It says nothing about living together.
Then, why do all couples do it?
Or do they all?

How We Got Here

Aaron and I met in 1998. He was the man of my dreams, but dreams are odd. Sometimes they start out joyfully and then turn into nightmares. Ours didn't, but it could have. "Living apart together" is the way we made things come out right for us.

We were both middle-aged when we found each other. We had a long-distance relationship for several months, and then decided to live together. Since he was moving to my town, I agreed to find us a place to live, and asked what kind of place he'd like.

He emailed me a staggeringly long list of requirements, right down to the carpet color. Trying to feel optimistic, I set out apartment hunting.

The only place I found that met our needs for space (let alone carpet color) was the whole top floor of an old fourplex apartment building. Both upper apartments were vacant, and they shared a utility room at the rear, so there were interior connecting doors. We decided to combine them into one unit.

I credit renting that place with saving our relationship. Because at the end of six months, we gave up. We could not live together. So we each took a unit, and barely spoke for the next month. Feelings were raw. It was obvious that one of us would move away before long, with an awkward goodbye, or none at all.

Neither of us wanted that. So we got together again, but this time, we didn't merge our apartments. At first, I felt disappointed. This was not what I had always imagined. I saw it as something he wanted, something I had to take or leave—"my way or the highway."

Then I realized that, for most of my life, I'd made major sacrifices to keep from having to live with a roommate. I'd often paid half my salary in rent. I'd abandoned the idea of saving for a down payment on a house. I'd lived in less-desirable houses and neighborhoods. I'd done whatever I had to do to be able to live alone.

So Aaron wasn't the only one who needed his own place. I still had misgivings, but I decided to give living apart together a fair try.

It worked so well that we went on that way for another several years. In the summer of 2004, we married. And we've lived happily apart together ever since.

Why was living apart together such a success for us? How can two people keep an intimate relationship going without cohabiting? Why would anyone even want to? Is this some modern breakdown of traditional marriage?

Surprisingly, there's nothing new about it. During the decades when I designed restorations for historic buildings, I was surprised to learn that a typical mansion is a large outer shell covering a collection of private apartments. Most have one suite for the husband and another for the wife, as well as a children's wing and one for servants. This is the way many couples live when they have all the choices in the world.

Some well-known people have chosen this arrangement—Fannie Hurst and her husband, Jacques S. Danielson; Arundhati Roy and husband Pradip Krishen; Jaimy Gordon and Peter Blickle; Deborah Moggach and Mel Calman; Helena Bonham Carter and Tim Burton. *New York Times* columnist Frank Bruni has written about his own separate but committed life with his partner.

So, is living apart together a "lifestyles of the rich and famous" kind of choice?

Not really. It's more *talked* about in the case of famous people because *they're* more talked about. But it's not uncommon for couples to live apart—from necessity or choice, temporarily or permanently. It isn't even an all-or-nothing proposition. It's something any couple might consider trying, in whole or in part.

Living apart together has even been discovered by social researchers—a 2013 article in the scholarly *Journal of Communication* featured a comparison of cohabiting and noncohabiting couples. The next knock at our door may not be a kid selling chocolate bars for the local school—it may be a sociologist with a clipboard.

This book will talk about the reasons and benefits—as well as a few disadvantages—that come with making conscious decisions about what to share and what to keep separate, both from our experience and from that of other couples we've met along the way.

It starts with a house tour—a look at each room, or type of room, in a typical house or apartment—and goes on to examine common drawbacks of combining two people's needs in such spaces and how an apart-together living arrangement might work better. After the tour, we discuss a few intangibles like housework, expectations, and compromise, as well as hot topics for many marriages, such as children, pets, and money.

And finally, the reason for it all: our precious time together.

Living Room

(Decorating and Entertaining)

"My husband's favorite chair was as tacky a piece of furniture as I've ever seen. So I got him to move it to the room he used for a home office. But then he started sitting in there after dinner, because he wasn't comfortable in any of the other chairs. So I did, too, and now no one uses the living room. Our teenage kids call it 'the museum.'"

Aaron and I had a real argument about furnishings when we first moved in together. He wanted to center his large bookcase on a particular wall—almost the only place it would fit. But there was a problem. The front door was on that wall, and I always hang a special framed graphic beside the door: "Peace to all who visit this home."

I didn't care how anything else in the house was arranged, but that door blessing felt important on a spiritual level. The wall was just big enough to fit both the picture and the bookcase, but only if the bookcase was pushed all the way to the corner. Since the blessing was so important to me, Aaron yielded, but even I would have had to admit that it wasn't an especially pleasing look.

An awkward compromise. Depending on how many of those a couple has to make, a home could end up feeling like it didn't belong to either of them.

Style and décor affect the whole house, but differences about the living room may be especially controversial, since the appearance of our more public rooms affects how others see us.

This may be a major problem in later marriages, when both partners already have households set up the way they like. I know of one couple who almost reached the point of divorce over furniture. At the time they married, both had established households. One wanted to furnish their new house with beloved family pieces, supplemented with antiques. The other already owned first-rate, expensive modern furniture. They married without settling the point, and when I met them, they were on their way to getting *un*married because of it. I don't know what happened in the end, but what a waste!

Then there's the issue of rearranging furniture. I love to. I love designing a new layout, especially in the living room, and enjoy the fresh feeling of a rearranged room. Aaron hates it. He moves into a place, arranges the furniture to suit him, and doesn't change anything until he moves out.

Since we don't live together, we both laugh over my "recreational furniture rearranging," but if one of us had to yield on this one, it would be a source of conflict.

Particular pieces of furniture can make for complicated decisions. Bookshelves and their arrangement are one example. Some people arrange books by size or alphabetize them by author. Some arrange their bookshelves by subject. I've even heard of grouping books by the color of the cover. Unless you both agree to use the Dewey decimal system, bookcases can cause endless bafflement and disagreement.

This wouldn't be an issue for us, since we both organize books by size and subject. But we're different when it comes to CDs and DVDs. I grudge them shelf space, since I mostly listen to music on my iPod anyway, so I bought some CD albums and got rid of all the packaging for almost all my individual disks. Aaron enjoys the artwork and liner notes that come with CDs and DVDs enough to give them shelf space.

The television—both its sound and control of the remote—can be another issue. If one of you is a TV person and the other isn't, or one likes TV sports and the other doesn't, the living room can quickly become individual territory instead of a shared comfortable space. The same goes if one of you likes jazz, or rock, or classical music, and the other is uncomfortable with it.

Friends, guests, and entertaining may be confusing as well. There's a lot of potential for conflict there.

Limited privacy is part of that issue. It's hard to have a tête-à-tête with a friend if a third person is in and out of the room. Not everyone would mind if a spouse overheard a conversation with a friend or even joined it. But there's something special about having a private talk with a friend. Why should marriage mean that you never get to do that in your own home again?

It's also possible that the spouse may not *want* to hear private conversations that may be uninteresting or distracting. Or even embarrassing.

It's not even a given that a couple will *like* each other's friends. If that happens, and you share a home, how do you handle it? Does one partner grin and bear it, or hide out in a private part of the house? Are some friends going to be "outside friends" that you meet elsewhere? Do you give up on friendships with people who aren't compatible with your partner, too?

Another issue with entertaining is schedule. I'm an extreme day person. I'm longing for sleep by 8:00 in the evening. Aaron stays up much later. But if we lived together, he'd hesitate to have friends over at night, for fear of bothering me.

And it's not just a matter of visitors. Aaron likes to play musical instruments at night—but he'd feel reluctant to do that, too. I like to play music, but I'm a rank amateur, and shy about other people hearing me. If I had no private place to play, I'd give it up.

If you have a big enough house, you might have extra rooms that could handle conflicting needs. Many houses have special rooms for TV watching, or are carefully laid out so that noise in the living room isn't audible in the bedrooms. Of course, separation of personal spaces under the same roof is one version of living apart together. If the living room were the only place where conflicts occur, this slight degree of separateness might work.

But it isn't, and often, it doesn't. Let's go on to the kitchen.

Kitchen and Dining Room

(Cooking and Eating)

"Back in the day, the kitchen was the wife's. So was all the shopping, cooking, and dishwashing. I thought I'd be happy when my husband decided to learn French cooking. Ha. What a nightmare—it never occurred to me that French chefs have underlings to wash all the pots. Guess who got drafted for that role in our house . . ."

When I was a young woman, my mother and her friends grumbled about how much their husbands complained about food. The women considered this an example of male unreasonableness, and it might have been. But I wonder. How would it feel to be a permanent child at your own table? Eat what you're given, when it's served, and the only control you get is to gripe?

It's hard to share a kitchen. It may be harder with more egalitarian lives, but I'm not sure even that is true. I've shared kitchens with housemates. Sometimes we cooked independently and cleaned up after ourselves. Or we bought food cooperatively, with rotating turns cooking and cleaning. Both these systems can work if everyone plays fair, but would you want to spend your life keeping score?

Using the kitchen is only half of it, too. Go back a step—a kitchen is a complicated workspace. Who gets to decide how it's arranged if both people share the cooking?

Aaron and I have lived in four places where our apartments were identical. In every case, we set up kitchens that were about as different as they could be. If he used one set of kitchen cabinets for dishes, another for cookware, and a third as a pantry, it was certain my arrangements would be opposite. Our notions of order and process in a kitchen are poles apart.

I prefer using a dishwasher. He hand washes dishes—he won't use a dishwasher even if an apartment has one. I put all the dishes away. He keeps frequently used pots and dishes in the dish drainer for convenience.

And then, there's what's on the plates. Again, we have different preferences and needs. Aaron's a skinny guy who probably loses a pound if he blinks more than usual. I have to watch my weight. He has food allergies. I don't.

Some of the foods we like are the same—we occasionally eat together, and often order the same entree in restaurants. But some of our strong preferences conflict. I can't stand fish, even the smell of it; he loves salmon. I eat a lot of dairy products; he's lactose intolerant.

We eat at different times, too. I get up early, have a good breakfast, and more or less graze for the rest of the day. He eats less in the morning, more for lunch and dinner. If we tried to eat every meal together, we'd both be uncomfortable a good bit of the time.

So we usually eat alone. To some of our friends, this sounds lonely. I don't think so. When you're not locked into compulsory cooking, shared meals become a treat. We each have specialties—mine is pizza; Aaron's is omelets. We give each other certificates sometimes—"Good for one pizza with 24 hours' notice" or "Good for an omelet if someone has eggs." They're small gifts, like stocking stuffers.

I love to cook, and especially enjoy cooking for guests or making surprises and treats for Aaron. He gets cookies, sourdough rye bread, and freshly squeezed juice regularly, as well as occasional Sunday dinners or "just because" celebrations. Cooking gives me a deep sense of home—it's as far from duty as anything could be. I wouldn't trade what we have for anything, certainly not for dinnertime routine.

I also make all our soap—unscented for him, usually lemon or herbal for me. This, too, is a pleasure *because* it's optional.

Let's close the kitchen door, and go on to the bedroom.

Bedroom

(Sleeping and Sex)

"If you don't live with your husband, he's going to cheat on you!"

"When do you . . . I mean how do you . . ."

A generation ago, it might be whispered as a scandalous tidbit that a married couple had separate bedrooms. Today, it's seen as a good idea, even erotic. Do an Internet search on the term, and you'll find more positive articles than negative ones.

At the very least, many people sleep better alone. I'm a case in point—I've had insomnia since I was in my twenties. Some nights I toss and turn and barely get to sleep at all. Sometimes I wake up in the middle of the night for a couple of hours and struggle to get back to sleep.

And Aaron snores—not loudly, just enough to jerk me awake if I'm finally almost asleep.

He's prone to middle-of-the-night idea storms, as well. We'd drive each other crazy if we shared a bedroom regularly.

We'd both be uncomfortable for other reasons if we tried. I sleep best in a chilly room, with warm but lightweight covers. I keep my bedroom window at least cracked open, even on most winter nights. After a night in a warm, stuffy room, I wake with a headache.

Aaron likes his bedroom warm, with heavy covers. He'd freeze at the temperatures I like.

I've been asked, directly and indirectly, what in the world we do about sex. I think we do what all successful couples do—we've worked out what suits us. There are many possibilities, even if you don't live together. You can have hot dates. You can be spontaneous, if that's what you prefer. You're spending time together, and some of that will be time in the bedroom. It works for dating couples who don't live together, so why not for spouses?

Except for the advantage that petty roommate resentments aren't complicating your feelings for each other, sex is much the same for living apart-together couples as it is for anyone else.

As far as fidelity is concerned, if cohabiting couples never cheated, there would be a lot less divorce. Sure, a spouse with his or her own place might have a few more opportunities, but opportunities abound to the point where that's a drop in the bucket. Someone who's looking for a "bit on the side" will find a time and place—business travel, motel rooms, the other woman's or man's apartment. The old saying "Where there's a will, there's a way" applies to sex at least as much as anything else.

Either you can trust someone, or you can't. If you can, you don't need to see what they're doing every minute. If you can't, don't marry that person.

Let's take a look in the bathroom next.

Bathroom

"The bathroom was the library, as far as my husband was concerned. Since we only had one, that caused a few problems."

Bathrooms are the site of major conflicts about privacy and sharing. Of course, many homes have more than one. That's a good start.

But, apart from the obvious, how does each person expect a bathroom to function? Are the bathroom counters kept clear? What goes in the medicine cabinet? Who needs more space, and who gets it?

What should be stored in a bathroom? I hang clothes I'm going to wear again on hooks. I store extra supplies and towels for guests. I'm a soap-maker, and I keep dozens of bars of handcrafted soap to use or give away. I use lotions and creams on my skin, and conditioners on my hair, so I keep the bottles and jars handy.

Aaron doesn't do, or like, or want any of that. If he had to share my bathroom, my clothes, soaps, creams, conditioners—my *stuff*—would be nothing but clutter to him.

I like to dab lemon or lavender essential oil on a washcloth and hang it on a towel rack to scent the room. I'm fussy about cleaning my bathroom, and do some tidying and scrubbing nearly every day.

On the other hand, I'm cavalier about splashing water on the floor. When I get out of the tub, I track water all over the place. Aaron, who often walks around wearing socks but no shoes, didn't appreciate this habit of mine when we lived together.

He also likes to have the toilet paper hung on the spindle in a consistent way, while I don't care. I can see the advantage of doing it the same way every time, but I usually don't remember to follow through.

So neither of us would be all that happy with the other's ideas about order and tidiness in a bathroom.

Or about privacy and territoriality. When I have a place with two bathrooms, one is mine alone. No one else uses it. Aaron doesn't see it this way at all—in his place, he or anyone else is free to use the nearest one. Another issue that we'd have to negotiate if we tried to live together.

Since it's wise to pick your battles, the Battle of the Bathroom is a good one to avoid.

Now that we've done the house tour, what about some of the big issues? Habits, attitudes, expectations, arrangements—how does all this work?

Housekeeping

"My ex was a sweet man, but he was a slob. Never washed a dish, never put anything away. We both worked, and it got me down to get into second-shift housekeeping while he got to take it easy in the evenings.

"One day I said, 'I think a married couple ought to live in a duplex.' And he just stared at me. No way he would have gone for that."

If there's one dependable source of differences between roommates—any roommates—it's house-keeping. Things can get heated enough with casual roommates. But when you've signed up to spend your life with someone who thinks cleaning is something the fairies do for you at night, you can get bitter fast. On the other hand, when your beloved wants both of you to spend your free time keeping the house nearly sterile, life can start to look like a sentence of hard labor.

This is not conducive to romance.

You can hire someone to get the work done, but housekeepers don't come cheap, nor should they. Sometimes, hiring a cleaner just changes the argument from one of time and effort to a money argument. Not an improvement.

Estimates vary about the percentage of marital quarrels centered on housework, but almost everyone agrees it's substantial. Why is housekeeping such a problem when people live together?

Standards

No two people have identical standards. If one person wants to have "a place for everything and everything in its place," and the other wants free time and has a high tolerance for disorder, who gets their way? Being in a lifetime relationship with someone whose assumptions about housekeeping are different from yours can pose some interesting problems about how much at home you feel in your own home.

It's unlikely that any two people's expectations about housekeeping are going to match. We all learned, by good or bad example, how to keep house by watching how our parents did it. And this early learning makes for almost unshakeable assumptions about the right way to do things.

Which, in turn, can make for quarrels when you live with someone who didn't grow up with your parents.

It's also not only a question of perfectionism versus a more casual style. Aaron and I are both orderly people, but our sense of order is different.

Aaron is happy if his place is safe, functional, and efficient. I expect all that, but I want mine to look like a spread from an architectural magazine as well—and I'll sacrifice a little convenience for the appearance I want.

However, when organization isn't immediately visible—in a place like inside the refrigerator or in a drawer—odds are, he'll be more organized than I will.

Sometimes we're both organized, according to our own standards, but our methods of organization differ enough that it's a good thing we don't have to compromise. For example, I have a box for power supplies and rechargers for everything from my camera to the handheld carpet cleaner. This box has sub-boxes, and one electric gizmo goes in each sub-box. Each is labeled. A clear lid fastens over the top—rather like a small briefcase.

I love it—perfect order. I know where everything is, and the cords don't get tangled.

Aaron hates the thing. I'm not sure why. His power supplies and rechargers have at times been collected in what I call "the heap," a formless mass of gear and wire spaghetti that takes up an entire section of kitchen counter. For months after we moved to one building, I thought he wasn't through unpacking. But he does know where everything is, and I suppose it's handy to not have to get it out of a box. I couldn't live with "the heap" for two days.

Training

Some parents teach their kids how to take care of themselves, including learning how to shop for food, cook, do laundry, wash dishes, keep a kitchen clean, make a bed—the whole package. Some don't. Adults who weren't taught may assume that it's the partner's job to take care of all that, much as their parents did. The partner may not share that assumption.

Housekeeping holdouts may use their ignorance as a justification for their lack of involvement:

"You know how to do this, and I don't, so you should do it."

Or, "Mess bothers you, and it doesn't bother me, so you should be the one to clean."

This seldom goes over well.

Decisions, Decisions

Whose job, or whose turn, is it to take out the garbage? If it's my turn, do I wait until the bag is full, or do I need to take it out if the kitchen smells garbage-y? What goes in the garbage as opposed to the recycling? How often is the can washed and deodorized? What type of bags should I use?

That's just one area of consideration. There are many more. Housekeeping is complicated. Someone makes hundreds of decisions about how to do things. Someone follows through, or doesn't. Day after day, after week, after month, after year—someone chooses products, uses them, maintains them, replaces them, reevaluates them, disposes of them.

Does every decision have to be made cooperatively? That could take a lot of time and energy. But if I'm the one who chooses the vacuum cleaner, does that make it my job to vacuum? If not, does my partner get stuck doing a job with tools or products he dislikes?

Scheduling

I once shared a house with a woman who had a simple rule: we spent every Saturday cleaning. Our standards for housekeeping weren't different, but I wanted to do tasks as needed, not by the calendar. Since I wasn't satisfied to forgo other Saturday plans, I found another roommate.

That's fine if you're just roommates who don't mesh. It's another matter if the relationship is an important one.

Preferences

It's a sad fact that some of the necessary household jobs are ones that hardly anyone enjoys doing. It's another sad fact that most of those are the ones that have to be done the most often.

When roommates try to split jobs based on who does what well, or who prefers which job, it usually works out that no one is especially eager to clean the toilet. And that often means the person who does it is the one who has the least skill at wiggling out of jobs they don't want to do.

Of course, there are fairer ways around this. I once worked in an office where professional staff had to do the janitorial work. Each week, a job sheet was posted, and employees had to do five tasks each, their choice. There was just one catch: employees didn't sign up to do a job—they signed off that they *had* done it. That way, no one could promise to do all the easy jobs as soon as the list went up.

But what works for employees may or may not work at home. Agreeing on who is supposed to do what is likely to turn one partner into the enforcer, also known as a nag. Not good for relationships.

Is This about Sexism?

Not necessarily. When I mention that my husband and I share a duplex, I get mixed responses. Often, women are envious. The idea of not being expected to do all the housework is a new one, and it sounds good.

Men are less likely to think it's a good idea. But it's not fair to assume that all men, or even many men, regard a housework-free life as one of the perks of marriage.

In fact, the less-involved partner isn't always the man. That's the stereotype, but we're people, not stereotypes. I've known a number of women who had no idea about keeping house. I think it's best to avoid politicizing the issue at all—just note that no two people are alike, and that many people's assumptions about housekeeping bring them into conflict with people they live with.

Let's be honest: everything has its disadvantages. With housework, having your own place means you get to set the standards, make the choices, and do the work when you feel like it. But that power comes at a price. You also have all the work and all the responsibility, just like single people. You never have to nag anyone to take out the garbage— except yourself.

Money

"Money is the source of more marital disagreements and breakups than sex is."

I don't know who keeps count of things like this, but this truism may well be accurate. Money can be a major source of dissatisfaction.

Every couple needs to work this out, whether the partners live together or separately. In some ways, it's clearer when you live separately and keep separate kitchens. When Aaron and I first got together, we worked separately and both paid our own bills. If one of us picked up something at the market for the other, we at least offered repayment.

As we began working together in our publishing venture, we came up with another scheme.

Even as our expenses remained identifiably individual, our income became mutual. On the other hand, neither of us wanted joint-use checking accounts. What we worked out was for me to have a personal checking account based on an independent income source, and for him to handle our joint writing and publishing income account. I use a credit card billed to him for normal expenses, and use my own account for gifts, charities, and miscellaneous expenses. So our rent, food, car expenses, medical and dental expenses, and other necessities are paid out of business earnings, as are his incidental and discretionary expenses.

The separate nature of my checking account isn't because this is "my money" as opposed to "our money." It's for our convenience in avoiding money transfers between accounts.

I know other couples who have three accounts—one for each spouse, and one for joint household expenses, with contributions from both partners, sometimes prorated by income.

What's important is that both should have an equal voice in earning, budgeting, and spending.

Kids and Elders

"All very well if you don't have kids..."

I'm not an authority about raising children in apart-together households, because I haven't done it. But I have known one apart-together couple with kids. To make matters more interesting, there was a live-in grandmother.

The wife was a voice coach who worked at home; the husband was a doctor with a busy practice and irregular hours. They lived in side-by-side houses with a common fenced yard. I don't know where the kids lived, or if they had rooms at both parents' places. I didn't know the family well enough to ask. I think the grandmother lived with the wife.

It worked for them. I would have to admit, owning two houses is an expensive way to live, but that's the only disadvantage I was aware of. Clearly, to them, a "normal" life wasn't what other people thought they should be doing—it was what they were happy doing.

More power to that idea—there might be fewer divorces and less misery if everyone saw it that way.

Living apart together would be a challenge with small children unless the two living units had a connecting door. However, I can imagine that parents of new babies might appreciate it—they could take turns being the "away" parent at night. At least one of them would be able to sleep!

Separate households are also a possible solution to the challenges of blended families, where each spouse has children from a former marriage. Sometimes, families can merge without tensions, but often, different parenting styles conflict. If one spouse is stricter than the other, and each one's kids have adapted to their own parent's style, there's a big possibility of bitter differences. Living apart together would make "house rules" clearer for everyone.

Pets

"Love me, love my dog."

Well, maybe not.

When most couples got together right out of high school, or even right out of college, the issue of pets was easier to settle. Mostly, either one could reasonably expect to veto nonhuman roommates in a shared house.

It's not so easy with later marriages. What if one has a cat, and the other is allergic? What if one is afraid of the other's dog, parrot, or tarantula?

Most people would be reluctant to get rid of a pet to suit a potential human partner. But if you're determined to live together, there's no good answer. Forget the relationship? That would be a shame. Get rid of the pet? Not a good choice, either.

Maybe the best "pet" to ditch is the "pet idea" that you have to live together?

Expectations

"You might have a nice relationship of some kind, but it's not a marriage."

Expectations can cause serious problems for everyone. That's hardly a novel observation. The earlier they're formed, the more resistant they can be to change. We learn about marriage from our earliest childhood by watching our parents and our friends' parents.

And they may or may not have been happy. Sometimes kids know this, and sometimes they don't. I've known more than one mother who hid her unhappiness because she blamed herself for her marital misery and didn't want to "spoil it for my daughter."

The quote that leads this chapter comes from an elderly widow I knew well enough to know that her husband had been physically abusive—so much so that she was permanently disabled. But, to her, that was a real marriage. Not living in the same apartment, no matter how happy the relationship, wasn't.

Obviously, our expectations weren't the same. Not even close.

In much less extreme cases, people differ. I'm not suggesting that everyone should live as Aaron and I do, but that it's a good idea to keep an open mind about the balance of "together and apart" that works best for you.

We've had various arrangements in the places we've lived. Once, we lived a couple of blocks apart—that was too far. Another place, a two-story duplex, had an interior stair with only one door—at his level—and a cased opening with no door at mine. That was too close for me—I want my own door. We lived in a couple of places where we had no common walls or floor/ceiling, and learned that it was easier to negotiate noise with each other than with outsiders. Since different combinations of togetherness and privacy have worked better or worse for us, I'm sure it's something that would vary from one couple to the next.

But to do that, you have to stop listening so much to what other people—including your own child-self and teenager-self—and start thinking about what you really want. Now. Not what should work, or what you once dreamed of, but what you can comfortably live with.

And once you've decided that, don't listen to what anyone else has to say. How could other people know what's right for you?

Compromise and Cooperation

"Why don't you just compromise?"

"Why can't you cooperate?"

Somehow, the picture of a married couple choosing to live separately makes some people think we're unable to meet each other halfway.

Not true. We share a car. We've moved to several different towns in two states, always reaching a satisfactory agreement about what to do next. We work together in a small business.

We help each other in case of illness, and we volunteer to do convenient errands. "I'm going to the market. Anything you need?" is a common sort of question. We even do a little traditional, gender-role–based task swapping. I like gardening; he doesn't. He knows how to do car maintenance; I don't. I'm a lot handier with a needle and thread, and he carries objects that are too heavy for me. I make holiday and social meals; he updates and maintains our computers.

But the day-to-day compromises we'd have to make to live together would be both petty and constant. When we've had identical apartments and looked at the difference in the way we used them, we had to laugh. In a two-bedroom apartment, I'd choose one for my bedroom, the other for my office. His choice in his place would be opposite. Those two "identical" apartments would be as far from identical in use as it was possible for them to be.

It's frustrating to negotiate every tiny decision—where to hang my towel, where to put the trashcan, whether a microwave oven is a need or a nuisance. Bringing this kind of irritation into my life's most important relationship seems senseless. Why do we do it to ourselves?

Dominance and Deference

"Someone is having a captainish sort of day."

Rarely is a couple so well-matched that both partners share the same degree of drive to have their way. Usually, one defers to the other, except in matters of great importance. But this can be a source of building resentment on the part of the one who defers, where no single issue seems worth making a fuss over, but the total is greater than the sum of its parts.

Living separately balances power. In our case, Aaron tends to elect himself captain of the ship. But with territoriality on my side, I can push back effectively.

One example is the thermostat. He fusses over thermostats to a degree that sometimes makes me want to scream. But he's sure that getting the thermostat adjusted properly will make me much more comfortable. How can I scream at someone who's trying to be helpful? Not screaming doesn't do it, either, though. If I choke down my protests one day, the next day is likely to bring more of the same.

I finally found a polite way to say, "If I want your help, I will ask for it," and that got the message across. Especially since it's my apartment and my thermostat, and I don't mess with his thermostat when I visit him.

That brings up an important point. When you have separate places, you are, to some extent, a guest when you visit your spouse. A privileged guest, but still a guest. And guests are, or should be, on their best behavior, even as they're treated as honored and special.

I can't think of a better way to be with your spouse. Isn't marriage a state of being a guest—and a host—in your partner's life?

Time Alone

"I love my husband dearly. But sometimes I just can't stand having him around."

A need to sometimes be alone is probably more common than many people admit, especially if they're in a valued relationship. It's a serious, visceral need. To have to give it up for your whole life would be a particularly harsh sentence. So would doing without love and companionship.

People have innate needs for both community and privacy. There are extremes at both ends, but for most of us, the two have to balance.

Aaron needs long periods of dependable silence, to be alone with his thoughts and ideas. I'm easily startled; it's very disconcerting to me when someone walks unseen into a room with me.

Both of us need time, space, silence, and a door, as well as the many things we need and get from togetherness. Living apart together, we don't have to choose.

Sometimes one partner's moodiness calls for time spent apart. Everyone has moods, and it's hard to keep them from affecting your partner when you don't have space and time to be alone. If one person is feeling frustrated or down, even if the other has nothing to do with the mood, it's hard to keep from getting entangled, feeling responsible, or trying to fix it.

And then there are quarrels, where both are contributing. Again, there's a lot to be said for cool-down space and time.

Privacy can be welcome also in cases of modesty. Not everyone is modest about bodily functions, the grosser aspects of illness, or similar issues. Some of us are. It's completely pointless to debate whether one should be ashamed of natural functions. Modesty is a feeling that doesn't go away because it's illogical or unshared.

In addition, depending on a couple's sexual arrangements, dressing and undressing may be seen as a come-on by one partner, while the other may not have meant to be provocative.

Time Together

"Why marry at all, if you're going to live apart?"

I've just written about seven thousand words rec-
ommending separate time and space for couples.
But time and space together are important, too.

If you don't live together, this doesn't happen
in the same way. You may have to do more plan-
ning. Depending on circumstances, unplanned
time may also be easy.

We have both. We work at home, and get together by plan every morning and every evening.
During the day, we drop in on each other from
time to time.

A typical weekday goes something like this: I
get up early, usually around 4:00 in the morning.
I get a fair amount of the day's tasks done early—
housework, some writing, or I might make bread
or a batch of soap. Aaron comes over around 7:30,
or whenever he wakes up. We sit and talk for about
fifteen minutes, maybe half an hour. Then we go
about our plans for the day.

We usually get together briefly during the day.
I'll pick up a chocolate bar for him when I go to the
market, or he'll fetch my mail as well as his own.

Or a problem may come up with a book or some other project that we need to discuss.

In the evening, he comes over and reads to me for a quarter hour or so, usually from a children's novel. After that, we curl up together. This is a special time, one that most of my women friends envy. We may discuss our day or various concerns, and we often nap. Then he goes home, and I go to sleep.

We spend more time together on weekends, including expeditions, matinees, and just enjoying each other's company.

I'd say we spend about as much time together as most working couples, and all of it is "good time," when we can count on undivided attention and affection. And of course, with no need for discussion of housekeeping details and other fiddling sources of disagreement, it's all the more enjoyable.

To answer the question at the head of this chapter—why marry if you're going to live separately—apart-together couples marry for the same reason anyone else does. After all, it's no longer usual for people to marry to justify living together. Many, many couples live together *without* marrying.

No, for us, marriage isn't the gateway to living together. We married for the big reasons that we also share with cohabiting couples. Love. Commitment. Companionship. All the same reasons, the same feelings. Different postal addresses are a trifle compared to that.

The Choice

If there were just one way for people to be married, and that was what everyone automatically wanted, it would be so convenient! Everyone would know what to expect. Everyone would be happy.

There's not. It doesn't work. My point in this book is not that everyone should live apart together. It's that it's a good idea to consider all possible choices.

There are degrees, too. One couple might be happy with sharing everything except that they want separate bathrooms or separate bedrooms. Or each might want one private space in a shared home—a workshop, a sewing room, *something*. Others may decide that the whole idea of together and apart is for them, or that it's not for them.

Let me leave you, then, with one idea—think carefully about your wants, hopes, and needs in your marriage. Be open to doing what works for both of you, whether it's conventional or unique.

And whatever that turns out to be, I wish you the best of luck.

Frequently Asked Questions

Don't you miss waking up together?

Since we both sleep badly and wake at different times, this wouldn't be one of our particular joys, even if we did live together. But if sleeping and waking together is special for you, I'd suggest carving out whatever separateness you need by finding it in other areas.

Is this as expensive as it sounds?

Probably you couldn't live this way as cheaply as a couple that shares rent. On the other hand, the way people spend their money is a big picture that reflects their priorities. We don't take, or need, long vacations, for example. One reason for that may be that we don't build up stress all year that has to be discharged by getting away.

Sometimes, people will say they wish they could live like we do, and then go on to say they're thinking about divorce, since they can't live together. But it's more expensive to divorce! In addition to the cost of separate establishments, you'll have the legal costs!

Keeping two households sounds environmentally irresponsible. There's no way you're not consuming more energy than if you shared.

When it comes to questions like this, I think you have to consider all of what you're doing. Aaron and I "lighten our footprint" in some significant ways, such as choosing not to have children. Another is that we share a car and work at home rather than commute. It's not all that useful to look at one isolated aspect of anyone's life.

This doesn't sound like a committed relationship. It would be so easy to go back to being single.

The divorce statistics of living-together couples don't speak well for that choice being much of an impediment to splitting up. Commitment happens in the heart and mind. I don't think convenience has a whole lot to do with it.

Is this just another way of saying "open marriage" or playing around? It sounds juvenile.

Not at all. Marriage is on the honor system in any event. If people want to cheat, they're going to, regardless of the living arrangement. If they don't, they won't, regardless of who is or isn't looking.

What's new about this? We've always had commuter marriages, military marriages, traveling salesman marriages, trucker marriages, and so on. Also, couples who can't get along have always lived apart, sometimes in a legal separation, sometimes not.

All true, but not what we're talking about. What we've done is choose to live close, but separately, for no reason other than that's what's best for both of us and for our marriage. It's a conscious choice, not something that's been forced on us.

What if one of you becomes sick or disabled?

If that happens, we'll do what works best for us, backed by the years of love and respect that have gone into our choices so far. And that's the main point I'm making throughout this book: Take a clear-eyed look at what you as a couple want, need, and consider best for you. And go with that. *Always* go with that, no matter what anyone else says. It's your life, your love—it belongs to you, and no one else.

ANNE L. WATSON is the author of a variety of works, including literary novels, soapmaking manuals, and a cookie cookbook. She is also retired from a long and honored career as a historic preservation architecture consultant. Anne "lives apart together" with her husband, fellow author, and publisher, Aaron Shepard, in Friday Harbor, Washington. You can find her online at **www.annelwatson.com**.

Also of interest . . .

THE GENTLEMAN'S HANDBOOK

A Guide to Exemplary Behavior
OR
Rules of Life and Love for
Men Who Care

Aaron Shepard

CPSIA information can be obtained
at www.ICGtesting.com
Printed in the USA
BVOW09s1143250517
485049BV00001B/10/P

9 781620 355091